THE LITURGICAL GOSPELS

THE
LITURGICAL GOSPELS

BY
W. H. FRERE, D.D.
of the Community of the Resurrection

WIPF & STOCK · Eugene, Oregon

Wipf and Stock Publishers
199 W 8th Ave, Suite 3
Eugene, OR 97401

The Liturgical Gospels
By Frere, W. H.
ISBN 13: 978-1-61097-003-7
Publication date 1/24/2011
Previously published by A. R. Mowbray, 1913

PREFACE

THIS little tract represents the utilization for a practical and restricted purpose of some results of a study of Latin Gospel-books, carried on now for some time and over a considerable area. The investigation is not yet completed, though it may be said hopefully that it is nearing a stage in which some tentative results that emerge from it can be put forward, which may carry further the work that has already been done by Tommasi, Pamelius, Zaccaria, Ranke, and more recently by Dom Morin and Fr. Beissel.

Meanwhile certain conclusions to which the writer has been led may be utilized for the purpose which this tract has in view, viz. the improvement of the series of Liturgical Gospels provided in the Prayer Book. It must be left to a later publication, and one of a technical sort, to justify the main conclusions, which are here assumed, as to the origin and history of the *Capitulare Evangeliorum* ; and also to modify them in some minor details, which are not germane to the present purpose, but will need to be taken into account in any fuller and more scientific dissertation. In the interim the indulgence of the scholarly reader is asked for much herein contained which is only roughly stated, and, as yet, unproved.

W. H. FRERE.

CONTENTS

SECTION		PAGE
1.	THE SOURCE OF THE GOSPELS OF THE PRAYER BOOK, AND THE ENRICHMENT NEEDED IN THEM	1
2.	THE SCOPE OF THE *CAPITULARE*, AND WHAT IT OFFERS FOR ENRICHMENT	3
3.	ENRICHMENT OF CHRISTMAS DAY	6
4.	VIGILS, EMBER DAYS, AND LENT	9
5.	HOLY WEEK	11
6.	EASTER DAY AND WEEK	14
7.	WHIT WEEK	16
8.	THE SUNDAYS AFTER TRINITY	17
9.	THE SUNDAYS AFTER EPIPHANY	19
10.	WEEKDAY GOSPELS	20
11.	ROGATION DAYS	22
12.	SAINTS' DAYS IN GENERAL	23
13.	DIRECT CONTRIBUTIONS FROM THE *CAPITULARE* TO THE PRAYER BOOK OF THE FUTURE	25
14.	FURTHER CONTRIBUTIONS FOR LATER FESTIVALS (RED LETTER DAYS) FROM THE OLD ENGLISH DIOCESAN USES	26
15.	THE ENLARGEMENT OF SUCH GOSPELS	28

Contents

SECTION		PAGE
16.	Black Letter Days from the same sources with Proper Gospels	29
17.	The Utilization of the Medieval *Common of Saints* for further Festivals	31
18.	The Material available and its Disposition for our Purposes according to the Precedent of the English Diocesan Uses	34
19.	The Use of this Material for other Festivals where there is no such Precedent	40
20.	Summary as regards Black Letter Days	42
21.	Gospels for some Votive Masses	44
22.	Conclusion	45
	A List of Lesser Festivals	46

THE LITURGICAL GOSPELS

§ 1

THE Gospels of the Book of Common Prayer are derived from an ancient Roman list, or *Capitulare Evangeliorum*, which in its earliest form belongs to the seventh century. No MS. of its primitive condition survives; the earliest that is extant seems to belong to the first half of the eighth century. But a comparison of the large number of copies of the list, that survive in Gospel-books ranging from that date to the eleventh century, shows plainly the character of the original nucleus; for there is a nucleus which persists throughout, unchanged in any essential respect, while new features are being gradually added, which vary in more or less degree, and vary increasingly in proportion as they belong to later stages of development.

It is proposed to examine the series of Gospels included in the Prayer Book, testing it primarily by these early lists; and where that cannot be done, by the Service-books of the medieval English dioceses, which drew upon the old Roman material, incorporating it with little alteration, though with much addition. Further it is proposed, in the light of that examination, to see what change or enrichment is now desirable. Enrichment is the principal need; for there is no special gain in an excessive repetition of the same passages. As it is, the same Gospel is bound to recur as often as seven times consecutively in any ordinary week where no Holy Day intervenes; and the Saints' Days that have proper Gospels are very restricted in number. Enrichment therefore is the first thing to be considered. But incidentally in the course of the enquiry some points will emerge in which a change is desirable from the existing state of things.

Three sorts of enrichment have to be considered, —first that which is needed in the Seasons, and secondly that which is needed for Saints' Days. Besides there is the third question whether the ferial days of the ordinary part of the year should not have some special provision made for them, on the lines of the old system. The effect of such a change would be to secure the reading of a far greater part of the Four Gospels at the Eucharist than at present, and this in itself seems very desirable. The first two questions, however, have a prior claim to consideration: and we shall chiefly concern ourselves with them.

So far as the Seasons are concerned, enrichment is chiefly required for (1) the weekdays in Lent, (2) the Ember Days, (3) the Rogation Days, (4) for additional celebrations on Christmas Day; (5) for the weekdays after Easter Day and Whitsunday; (6) for the Dedication Festival, Harvest Festival, and the like, and (7) for Funeral, Marriage, and other occasional offices.

§ 2

WHEN we turn to the *Capitulare* to see how far it can meet such requirements, we find that in its primitive form it seems to have made provision for the following papal services: three Masses of Christmas Day; the three festivals following, the Sunday following, and the Octave; the Vigil and Festival of the Epiphany; ten Sundays after Epiphany besides Septuagesima and the two following; Ash Wednesday and the Friday following; the remainder of Lent, except (*a*) the Thursdays up to Passion Week, and the Second Sunday, for on those days no solemn stational service was held in Rome; and (*b*) the Saturday before Palm Sunday and the Thursday in Holy Week, because on those days a peculiar service took the place of the usual one, and no provision therefore was made in the ordinary *Capitulare*. Provision was made for one Mass on Easter Day and for each day in Easter week; for the *Pascha Annotina*, or anniversary of the previous Easter, and for Low Sunday; for the Great Litany on April 25; for the remaining five Sundays after Easter up to Whitsunday with the Vigil and Festival of the Ascension. Whitsuntide had its Vigil, its Feast, and the ensuing Monday, Tuesday, Wednesday, and Friday provided for. Then followed a set of twenty Sundays corresponding to those which we reckon after Trinity, and four more which we reckon as Advent. Provision was probably also made for the three other Embertides, one soon after Whitsuntide, one in September, and one in Advent; and the series closed with the Vigil of Christmas.

The provision for Saints' Days was not set on a separate list, but interwoven with the provision for Seasons. It included a number of local Roman festivals which are not in our Prayer Book Kalendar; and there is a considerable number even of our Red Letter Festivals which it did not include.

Leaving the question of the Saints' Days for discussion later, we consider the above list. It meets very fairly the list of requirements made above: and indeed it does not seem unreasonable to suggest that all these days which were provided with a Gospel in the old *Capitulare*, so far as the Seasons are concerned, should be similarly provided for now in our Prayer Book. The Sundays need not for the moment be in question, for our provision for them is almost complete,[1] though it agrees not with the earlier, but with a later form of the provision in the Gospel Books. The following occasions, however, are in question :—

Vigil of Christmas. Mt. i. 18-21.
Christmas, i. Lu. ii. 1-14.

---

[1] The Second Sunday after Christmas has no proper Gospel, but takes that of the Circumcision. This is according to ancient precedent. There is no suitable material available which is unused, so it is best thus to borrow.

The Liturgical Gospels

Christmas, ii. Lu ii. 15-20.
Vigil of Epiphany. Mt. ii. 19-23.

Friday before Quadragesima. Mt. v. 43—vi. 4.
First Monday in Lent. Mt. xxv. 31-46.
First Tuesday in Lent. Mt. xxi. 10-17.
First Wednesday in Lent. Mt. xii. 38-50.
First Friday in Lent. Jo. v. 1-15.
First Saturday in Lent. Mt. xvii. 1-9.
Second Monday in Lent. Jo. viii. 21-29.
Second Tuesday in Lent. Mt. xxiii. 1-12.
Second Wednesday in Lent. Mt. xx. 17-28.
Second Friday in Lent. Mt. xxi. 33-46.
Second Saturday in Lent. Lu. xv. 11-32.
Third Monday in Lent. Lu. iv. 23-30.
Third Tuesday in Lent. Mt. xviii. 15-22.
Third Wednesday in Lent. Mt. xv. 1-20.
Third Friday in Lent. Jo. iv. 5-42.
Third Saturday in Lent. Jo. viii. 1-11.
Fourth Monday in Lent. Jo. ii. 13-25.
Fourth Tuesday in Lent. Jo. vii. 14-31.
Fourth Wednesday in Lent. Jo. ix. 1-38.
Fourth Friday in Lent. Jo. xi. 1-46.
Fourth Saturday in Lent. Jo. viii. 12-20.
Fifth Monday in Lent. Jo. vii. 32-39.
Fifth Tuesday in Lent. Jo. vii. 1-13.
Fifth Wednesday in Lent. Jo. x. 22-38.
Fifth Friday in Lent. Jo. xi. 47-54.

Wednesday after Easter. Jo. xxi. 1-14.
Thursday after Easter. Jo. xx. 11-18.
Friday after Easter. Mt. xxviii. 16-20.
Saturday after Easter. Jo. xx. 19-31 or 1-9.

Vigil of the Ascension. Jo. xvii. 1-11.
Vigil of Pentecost. Jo. xiv. 15-21.
Wednesday after Pentecost. Jo. vi. 44-51.
Friday after Pentecost. Lu. v. 17-26.
Saturday after Pentecost. Mt. xx. 29-34.

Ember Days of September :
  Wednesday. Mk. ix. 16-29.
  Friday. Lu. vii. 36-50 or v. 17-26.
  Saturday. Lu. xiii. 6-17.

Ember Days of Advent :
  Wednesday. Lu. i. 26-38.
  Friday. Lu. i. 39-47.
  Saturday. Lu. iii. 1-6.

We are now able to see more clearly how far this list of Gospels available corresponds with the list already made of Gospels desired. So far as the Seasons are concerned, the correspondence is almost complete, and most of the material has only to be adopted bodily to fill the places as required. But there are points which require some further consideration.

§ 3

WE begin with a consideration of the enrichment needed for Christmas Day, when a number of Celebrations are usual and much material is available. Comparing the Prayer Book with the *Capitulare*, we notice that the old Gospel of the second Christmas Mass is used in the Prayer Book

for the Circumcision (Lu. ii. 15-20), after having
annexed to itself the short medieval Gospel of that
day, which consisted only of a single verse, Lu. ii
21. In earlier days this Gospel had not been so
short, for the passage assigned in the early forms of
the *Capitulare* to the Octave of Christmas had
been Lu. ii. 21-32, and it was only later curtailed
to a single verse. The curtailment was probably
due to the adoption of the festival of Candlemas;
for then, a new Gospel being needed, twelve of
the thirteen verses were taken away from here to
serve there.

This festival has for its Gospel in the Prayer
Book Lu. ii. 22-40, that is the old Gospel of
Candlemas together with verses 33-40, which in
the ancient scheme belonged to the Sunday after
Christmas; while that Sunday has Mt. i. 18-25,
the first four verses of which belong in the old
scheme to the Christmas Vigil.

The situation may be expressed in tabular form
thus :—

PRAYER BOOK	CAPITULARE
Mt. i. 18-25, Sunday after Christmas.	Mt. i. 18-21, Christmas Eve.
	„ 22-25, First Mass of Christmas.
Lu. ii. 1-14.	
„ 15-21, Circumcision.	„ 15-20, Second Mass of Christmas.
	„ 21, Circumcision.
„ 22-40, Candlemas.	„ 22-32, Candlemas.
	„ 33-40, Sunday after Christmas.

The rearrangement of material thus made in
the Prayer Book is in itself exhaustive, except

that it leaves Lu. ii.1-14 free and unallotted. This passage therefore may well be used as an additional Mass on Christmas Day, as in fact is the case in the American Prayer Book; and perhaps with this additional provision we may rest content.

The old scheme, however, provided three Christmas Masses, one for midnight, one for twilight, and one at daylight; and some may wish to restore this. The midnight Mass is, however, a matter of doubtful expediency. It was never intended to be a late evening service, after which people went home to bed; it was the beginning of Christmas Day. If it were likely to be observed according to this intention, there would be something to be said for its recovery. But there seems no tendency for worshippers to show such Christmas devotion as to begin their Christmas at midnight and continue it right ahead; and failing that, the decadent substitute of a Christmas Mass, which is only a misplaced Evening Communion, is much to be deprecated.

The rearrangement of the material which the Prayer Book has effected is, however, not very satisfactory so far as the use of the passage in St. Matthew is concerned. This Gospel is not suitable for the Sunday after Christmas, and it is suitable for the Vigil. It would be better therefore to restore it to its old position there, perhaps in the fuller form (vv. 18-25) rather than the old shorter form (vv. 18-21). It will then be very simple to divide again the two ancient

Gospels which have coalesced to form the present Gospel for Candlemas, setting Lu. ii. 22-32 for Candlemas, and vv. 33-40 for the Sunday after Christmas, as of old. The gain of such a restoration will not only be a recovery of the old plan, but a more intelligent use of the Scriptures.

§ 4

LENT, Easter-week, and Whit-week are times in the year when it is most desirable that weekdays should have Scripture lessons of their own.

(1) The ancient scheme for Lent sets down a Gospel from St. John for all the days from Friday in the third week to the end of Passion Week, Sundays as well as weekdays. Beyond this fact, there is little to account for the choice of the particular passages. But whatever may have been the motives which dictated the arrangement, there it stands available for present use; and everything is in favour of recovering it as the additional provision now needed for Lent.

The ancient scheme is, however, incomplete, partly because there were no stational Masses at Rome on the Thursdays in Lent until the time of Gregory II († 731), and partly because of the other interruptions to the series which have already been mentioned above. We have therefore to consider also the best way of filling up these gaps. In all the existing Gospel-books except the very earliest some provision for most of these days has already been made. We consider the

Thursdays first. The morrow of Ash Wednesday is provided with Mt. viii. 5-13 as its Gospel: this clashes with the Third Sunday after the Epiphany, but there is no rival claimant, so it had better be taken. On the other Thursdays many alternatives present themselves. The three English Uses of Sarum, York, and Hereford agree for the most part and follow a little group of MSS. which gives the following series :—

Thursday after the First Sunday, Jo. viii. 31-47.
Thursday after the Second Sunday, Jo. v. 30-47.
Thursday after the Third Sunday, Jo. vi. 27-35.
Thursday after the Fourth Sunday, Jo. v. 17-29.
Thursday after the Fifth Sunday, Jo. vii. 40-53.

It will be noticed that all these are taken from St. John: they are also passages which were adopted as not being in use at any other place in the year: so for both these reasons they are very acceptable. The chief rival series to this (for these Thursdays) is one found in a much larger number of MSS.: but in this the Gospels are drawn from two different evangelists; they interrupt the series of Johannine Gospels in the later part of Lent, the last four being taken from St. Luke; and besides they are all borrowed from some other place in the series and therefore occur in duplicate. On all grounds therefore the Johannine series is to be preferred.

The two Saturdays in Lent which showed gaps in the earliest books were much less satisfactorily filled up. The first Saturday is still left without a Gospel in most of the later Gospel-books of our period. The MSS. which fill the gap at all are mainly those of the small group already mentioned. They give Mk. vi. 47-56, which came from the Sixth Sunday after the Epiphany when no longer needed there : this was adopted in the three English secular uses, and is therefore the best for our purpose. Similarly in the case of the Saturday before Palm Sunday there are many of the MSS. which leave the gap unfilled. The larger number of those that fill it up use for the purpose Jo. xvii. 1 to 11, or 15, or 26, which clashes with the Vigil of the Ascension; a smaller number, belonging to the group followed in England, use Jo. vi. 53-71 ; and there are half a dozen or more other passages less commonly used. It will again be best to follow the secondary group and take Jo. vi. 53-71.

The same remarks apply to the Second Sunday in Lent; here again great variety reigns. The English books, however, followed the same small but well-defined secondary group of MSS. in having Mt. xv. 21-28, a Gospel borrowed from the 10th Sunday after Epiphany of the primitive scheme. This was taken as being no longer needed for its old position, and it may well therefore be still adopted to fill this gap.

§ 5

WE come now to Holy Week. The *Capitulare* in its earlier form had no Gospel for the Thursday (since the day had no ante-communion service), but only the rubric *Ad Lateranis conficitur chrisma.* The St. Matthew Passion was read on Sunday, St. Luke on Wednesday, St. John on Friday. The Gospels of Monday and Tuesday were taken from St. John, being xii. 1-36 and xiii. 1-32 respectively. When a Gospel was wanted for the Thursday, that of Tuesday was adopted in whole or in part (1-15), probably because of the account that it contained of the Maundy. In many books the passage was thus twice read in the week : but some MSS. avoided this result, either by dividing Monday's Gospel into two and reading the second half on Tuesday, or by prescribing the St. Mark Passion to take the place left vacant by the transference of Tuesday's Gospel to Thursday ; or by dividing Tuesday's Gospel, taking only the first 15 verses to Thursday and leaving vv. 16-32 at Tuesday.

Of these expedients by far the most satisfactory is the adoption of the St. Mark Passion for Tuesday and the transference of the Tuesday Gospel to Thursday. It was not the most common, but it was the one which our English secular uses followed.

The Prayer Book exhibits a different scheme for Holy Week, which is evidently the result of a desire to shorten the Gospels. St. Matthew's Passion is retained at Palm Sunday, but only the later half of the old Gospel (Mt. xxvii. 1-54 instead of xxvi. and the whole of xxvii.). St. Mark is divided between Monday and Tuesday, but only vv. 1-39 of chap. xv. instead of the whole. St. Luke is similarly divided between Wednesday and Thursday and the end of the second of the two chapters of the Passion (xxiii. 50-56) is not read. The second of the two chapters forming the Passion according to St. John is read on Good Friday, but only as far as the 37th verse. The result of this is that Jo. xii. and xiii. are not read at all; and as regards the Passion, the account of the Maundy is read on Maundy Thursday at Evensong instead of at the Eucharist. The former of the two chapters, forming the Passions according to St. Matthew and St. John respectively, are read at the Mattins preceding, on Palm Sunday and Good Friday respectively; the various accounts of the Burial, which are docked at the end of the various Passions, are represented by the Gospel of Easter Even, which is Mt. xxvii. 57-64 (end). The old scheme provided in this place an Easter Gospel, Mt. xxviii. 1-7; for the service was a midnight service and belonged really to Easter Day. According to the old use the Saturday was free of services in the later part of the day, until the Easter Vigil began at night. Then in one long series came the primitive Vigil Service, the great Ceremonies, the Baptisms, the Confirmation, and the Vigil Mass, lasting through the night into Easter Morning.

This custom of keeping a real Vigil had vanished long before the Reformation; and it was better frankly to give up the idea than to retain an unreal survival. The ceremonies are divorced from their context when they are all anticipated, and occur on Saturday morning—as is constantly the case now according to the Latin Rite ; and the crisis of Easter is ruined. The Prayer Book is wise in making Easter Even the day on which to commemorate our Lord's burial ; and by keeping on that note till the Evensong of the Saturday, it does its best to reserve the unique transformation, for which Easter Day stands, until the Day itself dawns. No one will wish therefore to give up this—indeed it needs safeguarding against ill-advised attempts to make the Saturday Evensong a festival service : and the only modification that seems needed is the addition of two verses, Mt. xxvii. 55, 56, to the Sunday Gospel, for at present they have unaccountably fallen out in the dividing of that chapter between Palm Sunday and Easter Even.

§ 6

WE come now to Easter Day, where the Prayer Book gives as Gospel Jo. xx. 1-10. It is strange to notice that apparently this passage was not used in the earliest form of the *Capitulare*. The Gospel for Easter Day was from St. Mark. However, in early days a change was made which brought in the Johannine Gospel (Jo. xx. 1-9) for the Saturday in Easter week. The reason of the change was that the later verses of this chapter were being used twice over, vv. 19-31 on this Saturday and vv. 24-31 on the following day. This repetition was obviated either by taking only vv. 19-23 for Saturday ; or by adopting for Saturday the beginning of the chapter xx. 1-9. It will probably be thought best not to change the Easter Day Gospel of the Prayer Book : in that case it will be wisest to follow the former of the two rival precedents, *i.e.* to set down Jo. xx. 19-23 (the present Gospel for Low Sunday) for the preceding day, and Jo. xx. 24-31 for Low Sunday. The Prayer Book already has the old Gospels for Monday and Tuesday : and it is easy to add those for Wednesday, Thursday, and Friday, dealing with Saturday as suggested. The week will then be filled, and this is a very desirable piece of enrichment.

But Easter Sunday itself wants enrichment: it would be a distinct gain to have one or more alternatives provided. The old Gospel from St. Mk. xvi. 1-7 should be set alongside with the present Prayer Book Gospel, as in the American Book, perhaps with one additional verse ; and it will be a gain to take here also the old Vigil Gospel as a third alternative. The story of the Resurrection will then be read, in churches where there are three celebrations, from St. Matthew, St. Mark, and St. John. The story according to St. Luke will not be read. In some of the old lists it was added as an alternative on Low Sunday, in others it stood for Wednesday in Low Week. It might be well to recover it in one or other position. The second Gospel provided in the old scheme after Low Sunday for the anniversary of the previous Easter (*In Pascha annotina*, Jo. iii. 1-15) is now in use at Trinity Sunday, so it is not needed here.

§ 7

THE case of Whit-week is not so parallel to that of Easter-week as it appears to be at first sight. It is now habitually associated with the Ember Days, and this was so in the oldest Gospel-books; later an attempt was made to keep for the Octave its festival character by putting the Ember Days in one of the weeks following. The older usage, however, finally prevailed and the great fast of the fourth month asserted itself over the Octave. There is an appropriateness in each alternative. It was natural, when the idea of an Octave for Whitsunday arose, to wish to keep it in festival guise, and to exclude the fast; while on the other hand, ever since ordinations have been linked with the Ember festivals, it has been suitable that they should be closely linked with the festival of the Descent of the Holy Spirit. We are not likely now to wish for a change. That being so, the Wednesday, Friday, and Saturday will be provided with the Embertide Gospels, viz. Jo. vi. 44-51, Lu. xi. 17-26, and Lu. iv. 38-43; and the week will then be filled with the exception of the Thursday. Most of the early Gospel-books provide nothing for that day; but the secondary group, followed by our English uses, took Lu. ix. 1-6 when it was no longer required at the Eighth Sunday after Epiphany. It will be wise therefore to adopt this for the Thursday.

§ 8

WE come now to consider the Sundays : and though change in the existing provision of the Prayer Book is a very different thing from addition and enrichment such as we have so far chiefly considered, and is for the most part to be deprecated, it may be well to set out the case in brief.

The Sundays from Septuagesima to Pentecost (except the Second in Lent, which has already been discussed) offer no difficulty. The tradition is uniform and the Prayer Book follows it. Similarly the four Sundays before Christmas and the Sunday after it, though the former are not old Roman Stational Masses, are unchanged throughout. But the case stands otherwise with the *Dominicae vagantes*—those that fill up the variable intervening spaces that follow Epiphany and Whitsunday.

The oldest extant books provided 10 Sundays after Epiphany and 20 after Pentecost, to supplement the 22 already mentioned ; but the secondary group adopted a different plan, giving five only after Epiphany and 26 or even 27 after Pentecost. This plan is followed by our English uses and by the Prayer Book. In only one place is there any important divergence. At the eighteenth Sunday after Trinity there are the following five alternatives :—

(i) Mt. xxii. 23—xxiii. 12.
(ii) „ 34—xxiii. 12.

(iii) Mt. xxii. 23—46.
(iv) „ 23—33.
(v) „ 34—46.

Of these alternatives (i) (ii) are probably due to a mistake, for they each absorb the Gospel of Tuesday in the second week of Lent (Mt. xxiii. 1-12.); the alternatives therefore remaining are, either to read about the interview of the Sadducees with our Lord, or that of the Pharisees which followed, or both. The English diocesan uses agree in having only the interview with the Pharisees, and the Prayer Book follows them in this. There seems therefore to be no reason for any change.

In several instances in this series of Sunday Gospels, the addition of a verse or two is noticeable in the Prayer Book form of a Gospel, viz. at the 6th, 15th, 16th, 21st, 23rd, and 24th Sundays. In the last case the Gospel agrees with the York use, but is four verses longer than in the uses of Sarum and Hereford. In all cases but the first, the gain is unquestionable; the Gospel is carried on to the end of the section, and the additional verses thus incorporated were not otherwise utilised in the scheme of Gospels. But the two additional verses of the 6th Sunday form part of another Gospel, that of the Wednesday in the third week after Trinity; and the addition is so far open to question. Similarly at the 22nd Sunday two verses are prefixed: these are very appropriate, but they are part of a Lenten Gospel. The addition therefore is a questionable improvement.

§ 9

WE turn next to the Sundays after Epiphany, where the oldest tradition and the largest number of MSS have 10 Sundays, but the secondary group only 5. One might expect to find that the latter group had reduced its Sundays after Epiphany and increased its Sundays after Pentecost by transferring some Gospels from the earlier position to the later ; but this is not so, except in one case. The discarded Gospels of the Sundays after Epiphany were otherwise used up by the secondary group, as is shown below :—

Sixth Sunday becomes First Saturday in Lent.
Seventh Sunday
Eighth Sunday = Thursday in Whit-week.
Ninth Sunday = Twentieth Sunday after Trinity.
Tenth Sunday = Second Sunday in Lent.

It will be noticed that only in the last case but one does the sort of transference that might have been expected actually take place.

The first five Sundays of the set are uniform in all early MSS. Many of these give also an alternative Gospel for the Second Sunday, Lu. iv. 14-22. This series is reproduced in the English uses, except that York adopted at the 5th Sunday the alternative Gospel of the 2nd Sunday in place of the usual one. The Prayer Book has followed the ancient use for these five Sundays; except that, at the 4th, it has added to the old Gospel the remaining seven verses of the chapter (Mt. viii. 28-34). These verses are not utilized elsewhere in any normal form of the *Capitulare*, though they figure at Friday in the 22nd week after Trinity in the Hereford use and in at least one old authority. There is no need therefore to object to the addition.

A proper Gospel for the 6th Sunday after Epiphany was first provided in the Prayer Book in 1661. The medieval uses had been content with five, because it had become customary to keep the Sunday after the Epiphany as the Sunday in the Octave. The series of five then began with the following Sunday, and the Sundays were reckoned as Sundays after the Octave of the Epiphany, instead of Sundays after the Epiphany as before. In earlier days presumably the need was met by using the alternative Gospel usually provided at the 2nd Sunday. In the Prayer Book a return was made to the old plan, since no Octave was prescribed, but consequently the sixth Sunday could only borrow from the fifth. To remedy this defect a 6th Sunday Gospel was provided, and Mt. xxiv. 23-31 was taken for the purpose. This provision clashes with the arrangements made in some few early English Gospelbooks for the Saturdays in the 20th and 25th weeks after Trinity: but such clashing is of no great importance, and the Gospel may well stand as it is.

§ 10

THERE remains one question more to be discussed before passing from the Seasons to the Saints' Days, viz. whether it is desirable to add Gospels for the weekdays in Advent and Eastertide and in the times after Epiphany and Trinity, where such provision was formerly made, *i.e.* on Wednesdays, Fridays, and more rarely Saturdays. Apart from the Ember Days and Rogation Days the need for these is not great, compared with the need that there is for the occasions previously mentioned : and as the problem of the precedents is a somewhat intricate one, it will be best not to enter upon it.

In case, however, the problem should come up for discussion, it may be well to note in general, that, in these, as in other cases, not provided for in the original *Capitulare*, there is underlying the early MSS. a double tradition, which may be clearly made out, in spite of the many dislocations, confusions, and haphazard alterations that characterize the ferial Gospels as they appear in the early Gospel-books. (i) The older tradition, supported by most MSS., is that which goes hand in hand with the older and more widespread tradition already noted, in such cases, *e.g.*, as the provision of 10 Sundays after Epiphany and 20 after Pentecost. (ii) The secondary group appears again sharply contrasted with this; and the English uses, as before, follow it for the most part. In later documents the older tradition is found to borrow from the newer to fill up its gaps; and the two streams of tradition become confused ; but by going back to the earliest MSS., and studying them closely, the two traditions can be distinguished clearly from one another. For our present purpose there is no reason to go any deeper into this question—one of the most intricate that occur in the study of the Gospel-books; but if ever it becomes desirable to add to the Prayer Book further ferial Gospels for the year, this is the clue which will have to be followed, in order to reach a right decision as to the passages to be chosen for the purpose.

It may be noted also that until some such ferial Gospels are provided, a large number of valuable passages will never be read at the Eucharist—*e.g.* the account of the Baptist's preaching; of the Baptism of Christ (unless it is set for the Vigil or Octave of the Epiphany); of the Sabbath in the cornfield, of the rich young ruler, and many others from the synoptic record; besides passages peculiar to St. Luke—*e.g.* the Unjust Judge, the dinner in Simon's house, and Zacchaeus, unless set for the Dedication Festival.

§ 11

THE Gospels of the Ember Days of September and Advent have already been given above, for they form part of the early form of the *Capitulare*; but nothing has been said as to Rogation Days. The old Roman rogation was the *Litania Maior* on April 25; and in the earliest forms of the list this appears immediately after Low Sunday with Lu. xi. 5-13 as its Gospel. Later on two changes took place: (i) the Gallican Rogation Days, the three days before the Ascension, were adopted into many forms of the Roman site, and (ii) the 25th of April, the old Roman Rogation, was adopted as St.

Mark's Day. Consequently that day took a Gospel appropriate to the Evangelist, and the Rogation Gospel was transferred to the Monday before Ascension Day. The primitive scheme had only one Gospel for Rogations. One or two additional Gospels are, however, found provided in a few MSS.; they occur sometimes in the old Roman position and sometimes in the Gallican place, *e.g.* Lu. vi. 36-42 and Mk. xi. 22-26. The former is the more common of the two; but the latter (beginning at ver. 23) has English precedent. It is appointed for the Rogation Tuesday in the use of York, where Sarum provides nothing special, and Hereford has recourse to a still rarer selection, Mt. vii. 7-14. It is desirable that the old Rogation Gospel should be prescribed for the Monday, and one of the above for the Tuesday.[1]

§ 12

THE problem of the Saints' Days is one of a rather different sort. The greater part of those days which figure in the *Capitulare* do not reappear in the Prayer Book Kalendar; nor are they likely to be replaced in any future enlargement of that Kalendar, since they belong for the most part to obscure local Roman saints. At the same time they cannot be left out of account, for they provided the Gospels that later were assigned to

[1] The York Gospel reappears at Wednesday in the 22nd week after Trinity: but, if those ferial Gospels are not taken into account, that is no objection to its use here.

new names in the Kalendar which have survived—
and those Gospels, too, which, by a further development, came later to find a place in the *Commune
Sanctorum*, as suitable for a whole class of Saints.

The *Capitulare* in its early form knows nothing
of such a plan as yet. Every day has its own
proper Gospel assigned to it in the list: and
though the same passage may be used for several
Saints, the fact can only be discovered by a process
of comparison.

Following out this line, we may attack the
problem in two divisions: first setting down such
days with their Scriptures as are derivable direct
from the early form of the *Capitulare*; and second,
tracing the growth of the *Commune* and the addition of other Gospels which will be suitable for
days not included in the early list. In strict logic
such a procedure would first require a discussion
and settlement of the exact form of the Kalendar
as desired in a new edition of the Prayer Book.
But, without this, we shall find that the work can
be done roughly, leaving certain minor points to
be decided when the Kalendar is settled. For
the present it will be enough (1) to assume that
the present list of Red Letter and Black Letter
Feasts will continue, though without expressing
the opinion that they all necessarily should;
(2) that Gospels are to be found in some way for
all these days, and (3) also for a certain number of
additional days. The additions, which we shall
keep in view, are mainly those which have been
discussed or advocated already in the writer's *Some*

THE LITURGICAL GOSPELS 25

Principles of Liturgical Reform ; but there will be no need to cover exactly the same ground.

§ 13

THE list of days and their Gospels, occurring in the old *Capitulare*, and found in the existing Kalendar of the Prayer Book, or likely to be found in a future Kalendar, is as follows :—

ST. ANDREW. Vigil	Jo. i. 35-51.	
Day	Mt. iv. 18-22*.	
St. Lucy	Mt. xiii. 44-52.	*Simile thesauro.*
ST. STEPHEN	Mt. xxiii. 34-39*.	
ST. JOHN	Jo. xxi. 19-24 (to 25*)	
HOLY INNOCENTS	Mt. ii. 13-18* or 24.	
St. Silvester	Mt. xxiv. 42-47.	*Vigilate.*
St. Prisca	Mt. xiii. 44-52.	*Simile thesauro.*
SS. Fabian and Sebastian	Lu. vi. 17-23.	*Descendens Iesus.*
St. Agnes	Mt. xxv. 1-13.	*Simile decem virginibus.*
St. Vincent	Jo. xii. 24-26.	*Nisi granum.*
PURIFICATION	Lu. ii. 22-32 (to 40*).	
St. Agatha	Mt. xxv. 1-13.	*Simile decem virginibus.*
St. Valentine	Lu. ix. 23-27.	*Si quis vult.*
ANNUNCIATION	Lu. i. 26-38a (to 38b*).	*Missus est Gabriel.*
St. George	Lu. xxi. 14-19.	*Ponite in cordibus.*
SS. PHILIP and JAMES	Jo. xiv. 1-14*.	
ST. JOHN BAPTIST. Vigil	Lu. i. 5-17.	
Day	Lu. i. 18-25.	
	Lu. i. 57-68 (to 80*).	
SS. PETER and PAUL. Vigil	Jo. xxi. 15-19.	
Day	Mt. xvi. 13-19*.	*Venit Jesus in partes Caesareae.*
ST. PAUL	Mt. xix. 27-29.	*Ecce nos reliquimus.*
St. Peter's Chains	Mt. xiv. 22-33.	*Jussit Jesus.*
St. Lawrence. Vigil	Mt. xvi. 24-28.	*Si quis vult.*
Day	Mt. x. 37-42.	*Qui amat patrem,* part of *Nolite arbitrari.*
	Jo. xii. 24-26.	*Nisi granum.*
Repose of B.V.M.	Lu. x. 38-42.	*Intravit Jesus.*
Nativity of B.V.M.	Lu. i. 39-47.	*Exurgens Maria.*
SS. Cornelius and Cyprian	Lu. xi. 47-54.	*Vae vobis.*

MICHAELMAS	. .	Mt. xviii. 1-10.*
St. Martin	. .	Lu. xii. 35-40. *Sint lumbi.*
St. Cecilia	. .	Mt. xxv. 1-13. *Simile decem virginibus.*
St. Clement	. .	Mt. xxv. 14-23. *Homo quidam peregre.*

Some of the above are used for more than one occasion, and a Latin catchword is given to them in the list, for purposes of identification. The others are peculiar to the day.

The asterisk indicates agreement with the Prayer Book, and in some cases shows that the Gospel is longer there.

Such are the entries in the original *Capitulare* which chiefly need our attention; though, strictly speaking, it can hardly be said that the Festivals of the B. V. Mary in the above list are part of the old *Capitulare*. Candlemas has a Gospel taken from January 1: the Annunciation and the Nativity borrow from the Advent Ember Week, and the Assumption has the passage previously appropriated (with a slightly different opening) to St. Felicitas (Lu. x. 38-42).

§ 14

IT will be observed that this list makes no provision for eleven of the present Red Letter Days. They did not figure in the earlier lists, but they crept in by degrees; and most of them obtained a place in the tenth and eleventh centuries. But by that time uniformity has been lost, the list is being enlarged locally in many centres, and divergent traditions are arising. For some of these days half a dozen or more different Gospels are being prescribed before the end of the eleventh century in different lists. A choice must therefore be made as to which of the rival traditions should be followed. For our present purpose we choose the English tradition, as represented by the three best known diocesan uses of Sarum, Hereford, and York.

In most of these cases the three agree, and the Prayer Book follows more or less exactly the common tradition. Thus we have :—

1. St. Thomas . . Jo. xx. 24-29 (to 31*).[1]
2. St. Matthias . . Mt. xi. 25-30.*
3. St. James . . . Mt. xx. 20-23 (to 28*).[2]
4. St. Bartholomew . Lu. xxii. 24-30.* *Facta est contentio.*
5. St. Matthew . . Mt. ix. 9-13.*
6. St. Luke . . . Lu. x. 1-7.*
7. SS. Simon and Jude . Jo. xv. 17-25 (to 27*). *Haec mando.*
8. All Saints . . . Mt. v. 1-12a (to 12b*). *Videns autem Jesus.*

In the three remaining cases the Prayer Book follows Sarum :—

9. Conversion of St. Paul Mt. xix. 27-29 (to 30*). *Ecce nos reliquimus.*
10. St. Mark . . . Jo. xv. 1-7 (to 11*). *Ego sum vitis vera.*
11. St. Barnabas . . Jo. xv. 12-16*. *Hoc est praeceptum.*

Hereford differs in the first case, York in the second, and both in the third.

---

[1] The more common Gospel in the old sources is *Hoc est praeceptum*.

[2] The more common Gospel in the old sources is *Nihil opertum*.

§ 15

BEFORE we leave the existing Red Letter Days notice must be taken of the addition of verses to the Gospels made in the Prayer Book and indicated in the above tables. The case of Candlemas has been already considered. In most of the other cases the addition is a gain : *e.g.* the St. Mark's Day Gospel absorbs five verses of the xvth chapter of St. John, assigned of old to the Wednesday before Whitsunday; but this is no harm, unless they should be wanted in that capacity for insertion in the Prayer Book. The rest of the chapter is assigned partly to St. Barnabas (*Hoc est praeceptum*) and partly to SS. Simon and Jude. At the latter point the Prayer Book again adds verses beyond the limits of the old Gospel—viz. verses 26, 27, which belong to the Gospel of the Sunday after Ascension. This elongation therefore seems less justifiable.

At St. John Baptist's Day a more considerable elongation is found, for the old Gospel took in only one verse of the *Benedictus*, while the Prayer Book includes the whole. As the passage is not included in any other Gospel, this may be regarded as a gain. The same may be said of the addition of five verses to the Gospel of St James's Day. Similar additions at St. Thomas's Day, St. John's Day, the Conversion of St. Paul's and the Annunciation may be justified on the same ground ; but it must be admitted that in these cases they detract from the point of the selection, rather than add to it.

§ 16

WE pass on now to deal with further festivals, which it may be well to insert in the Prayer Book series. In some cases a proper Gospel is demanded because the day is directly connected with a scriptural passage; in others there is no such direct connexion, and the passages must be chosen on general grounds. To the former class belong certain days, which are set down here, together with the Gospel of each according to the *Capitulare*, or failing that the Sarum Use.

1. The Conception of the B.V.M. Mt. i. 1-16, the Genealogy.

The Festival was not in the *Capitulare*, nor perhaps is it needed in the Prayer Book. The Gospel was one of the alternatives for the Nativity of the B.V.M. (Sept. 8), and if it is replaced, would come better there. In old days the Genealogies were a special feature among scriptural lessons; they had proper and elaborate tunes of their own, to which they were sung. But it is doubtful whether, even if this musical treatment were recovered, they would be edifying in these days. It may therefore be preferable to choose, if required, for either of these days, St. Luke xi. 27-29—"Blessed is the womb," etc. This was in old days an alternative Gospel for the Assumption, but it forms part of the Gospel of the Third Sunday in Lent. The more usual though less appropriate alternative was Lu. x. 38-42, as has been mentioned above. This can be better employed, with good precedent, elsewhere: so for any of these three days, or all, the former excerpt seems preferable.

2. If St. Joseph's Day (March 19) is desired, there are obvious passages of Scripture specially appropriate; but there was no provision for this day made in the *Capitulare* or in any old English diocesan use.

3. Holy Cross Day (May 3). Jo. iii. 1-15, "Visit of Nicodemus."

This day and this Gospel are among the early additions to the *Capitulare*, and they are common to Sarum, York, and Hereford. But the passage belonged originally to the *Pascha annotina*, and was repeated by analogy at the Octave of Pentecost. It was subsequently kept in the later position to serve for Trinity Sunday, and figures there now. It may be well therefore instead to take here Jo. xii. 31-36, which is found at Sarum and Hereford for Sept. 14, the other Holy Cross Day (or to begin at verse 27 as in *The English Liturgy*), and thus to use the same Gospel on both days. This passage forms part of the old Gospel of Monday in Holy Week, which has been displaced by the Prayer Book rearrangement.

4. The Visitation (July 2), Lu. i. 39-47.

This is not an ancient use of this Gospel. It is merely taken over here from the Assumption, where it in turn was borrowed from an Advent Ember Day.

5. St. Mary Magdalene (July 22).

The later medieval uses had for Gospel the

passage (Lu. vii. 36-50) about the Sinner Woman. This is, to say the least, a hazardous choice: for the identification which dictated the choice is very unlikely. It is probably better to have some unquestionable record of the Saint read, *e.g.* Jo. xx. 11-18,—" Our Lord's appearance to her in the garden."

  6. The Transfiguration (Aug. 6), Mt. xvii. 1-9.
  7. The Name of Jesus (Aug. 7), Mt. i. 20-23.
  8. The Beheading of St. John Baptist (Aug. 29), Mk. vi. 17-29.

These call for no comment, and Holy Cross Day in September has been already discussed.

§ 17

THERE remains the large series of minor festivals —the present Black Letter Days and others to be suggested—for which there is no passage directly applicable; so that one must be sought with a more remote kind of appropriateness. The old *Capitulare* had no *Commune* : it gave for every day a reference to a particular Scripture. In many cases, however, such a Scripture was used for more than one Saint's Day; so that actually, though not obviously, some passages served for groups of similar days. The easiest example of this procedure is afforded by the days of Virgin Saints. For this group of days only two passages were utilized—the parables of the Treasure and of the Ten Virgins. The former is found at the feasts of St. Prisca, St. Agnes *secundo*, St. Pudentiana, St. Praxed, St. Sabina, SS. Lucy and Euphemia, St. Lucy; the latter at those of St. Agnes, St. Agatha, St. Cecilia, and at the old Roman feast of St. Mary at Christmastide (in early copies, but not the earliest, of the *Capitulare*). These two passages are therefore still the best ones to utilize for the said class. Thus the days of St. Lucy, St. Prisca, St. Agnes, and St. Agatha, among the older festivals recognized in the *Capitulare*, should continue to have the Gospels above mentioned; and among additions, St. Margaret of Antioch and St. Faith may well have the former, according to Old English use, and St. Bride, St. Perpetua, and St. Hilda the latter.

The Gospels allotted to other days present a more complicated problem. In the list given above (pp. 25, 26) a larger number of the Gospels are distinguished by Latin catchwords. They are, as has been noted already, those which were not peculiar to a particular day, but common to several days. They came therefore ultimately to form the *Commune*. But the process of the formation of the *Commune* was differently carried out in different places: and the common stock, when once formed, was differently utilized. For example, the Gospel *Qui vos audit* (Lu. x. 16-20) is peculiar in the *Capitulare* to St. Felix (Jan. 14); but when it comes into the *Commune*, York uses it for a Confessor, while Sarum and Hereford use it for a Martyr. It may be said, however, in general that the Gospels given in the

THE LITURGICAL GOSPELS 33

Capitulare for non-biblical Saints passed (with few exceptions) into the *Commune*, leaving only some of the biblical Saints to have proper Gospels.[1] One or two that did not pass into the *Commune* went out of regular use altogether. Thus in the case of Euplus (Jo. xvi. 20-23) both festival and Gospel went out of use[2]; again in the case of SS. Nereus and Achilles the old Gospel (Mt. xix. 3-11) went,[3] and another drawn from the *Commune* took its place.

The number of such Gospels contained in the *Commune* in English uses is about forty. Not all of these are available for Black Letter Days, but over thirty are. The number of Black Letter Days in the present Prayer Book Kalendar, apart from those already discussed, is between forty and fifty. It seems probable therefore that, so long as this proportion, between feasts requiring Gospels and passages available for them, is maintained, (and it is not likely to be much altered by any revision at present conceivable) there is no need for a large *Commune*. Most of the days can have a proper Gospel; others can be supplied easily by a cross reference. This, however, is a mere matter of arrangement and can be decided later. Our next step is to go through the Common Gospels, to note the original place of each and trace to what other

---

[1] And not all of them, for there was the Common of Apostles which took Gospels amongst others from St. Peter and Paul and the Commemoration of St. Paul.

[2] But this Gospel only formed part of two Gospels of Eastertide, those of the Third and Fifth Sundays after Easter.

[3] But part of it was used for Weddings: see below, p. 44.

F

festivals, among those for which we now have to provide, each was allotted in medieval days.

§ 18

WE may put this in tabular form, following for convenience the order of the Sarum *Commune*.

Ego sum vitis vera,[1] Jo. xv. 1-7 (or 9 or 11) originally for St. Vitalis or (1-11) for St. Hadrian. At Sarum for the Vigil of an Apostle, and for a Martyr or Confessor in Eastertide. Available for such a place—*e.g.* St. George, St. Richard, or St. Alphege, and actually in use at St. Mark.
Haec mando, Jo. xv. 17-25: originally for SS. Alexander, Eventius, and Theodulus, St. Pancras, SS. Cosmas and Damian, St. Chrysogonus. At Sarum for an Apostle. Actually in use at SS. Simon and Jude.
Ecce ego mitto, Mt. x. 16-22: originally for St. Sixtus, etc. (Aug. 6). At Sarum for an Apostle and for Martyrs. Available for SS. Crispin and Crispinian, as at Sarum.
Ecce nos reliquimus, Mt. xix. 27-29, originally for the Commemoration of St. Paul. At Sarum also used for the Conversion; and so actually in the Prayer Book.

[1] Sarum gives also as an alternative the last three verses of this passage, *Ego sum vitis, vos palmites,* Jo. xv. 5-7, for Martyrs and Confessors in Eastertide.

Venit Iesus in partes, Mt. xvi. 13-19, originally for SS. Peter and Paul, and later for St. Peter's Chair and Chains. So in Sarum, and actually on St. Peter's Day.

Facta est contentio, Lu. xxii. 24-30: originally for St. Apollinaris. At Sarum for St. Bartholomew: and so in the Prayer Book.

Designavit dominus, Lu. x. 1-7: not in the early *Capitulare*, but adopted for St. Luke, and so used in the Prayer Book. Sarum placed it in the Common of Evangelists, but used it also for St. Augustine of Canterbury out of Eastertide.

Nisi granum, Jo. xii. 24-26: originally for St. Vincent, St. Lawrence (3rd Mass), and St. Caesarius. Thence at Sarum in the Common of a Martyr. Now available for St. Vincent and St. Lawrence, the two Deacon Martyrs.

Qui vos audit, Lu. x. 16-20: originally for St. Felix; then at Sarum and Hereford for a Martyr, at York for a Confessor.

Si quis vult, Mt. xvi. 24-28: originally for the Vigil of St. Lawrence, while the similar Gospel, Lu. ix. 23-27, was used for St. Valentine, St. Mennas, St. Nicomede (Sept. 15); the former alone was used at Sarum for a Martyr; available for St. Valentine, St. Nicomede (June 1), and St. Alban.

Si quis Venit, Lu. xiv. 26-33 originally for SS. Timothy and Symphorian: thence at Sarum for a Martyr; and available for St. Oswald,

St. Edward, and St. Edmund—the three royal martyrs.

Nihil opertum, Mt. x. 26-32, originally for St. Cyriac ; then at Sarum for a Martyr, and available for St. Blaise. It is, however, only the latter part of *Cum persequentur* (below).

Circuibat Jesus, Mt. ix. 35-38 : not in the early *Capitulare*, but used at Sarum for a Martyr Bishop, and available for St. Lambert.

Homo quidam nobilis, Lu xix. 12-28 : originally for Pope Stephen ; then at Sarum for a Bishop martyred, or a Confessor in exile ; and thus available for St. Thomas of Canterbury and St. Brice. It also stands at Sarum for St. Machutus, and St. Clement ; but the latter has a different Gospel in the *Capitulare*.

Elevatis Jesus oculis, Lu. vi. 20-23 : not in the early *Capitulare*, but used by Sarum for Many Martyrs. It is only the latter part of *Descendens Jesus* (below), and so need not be treated separately.

Videns Jesus turbas, Mt. v. 1-12 : originally for The Seven Brothers, but used by Sarum for Many Martyrs. It became the Gospel of All Saints' Day, and is so assigned in the Prayer Book.

Cum persequentur, Mt. x. 23-26 : originally for SS. Protus and Jacinth, then for Many Martyrs, and utilised for St. Boniface and his Companions.

Ponite ergo in cordibus, Lu. xxi. 14-19 : originally for St. Theodore (Nov. 9), and later for St. George ; but taken at Sarum for Many

Martyrs and not used for St. George. For to that festival, coming in Eastertide, was assigned *Ego sum vitis vera*. The instruction of Our Lord which the Gospel contains is addressed to hearers in the plural, therefore there was some reason for the change. This Gospel is, however, only part of *Cum audieritis* (below) and need not be treated separately.

Descendens Jesus de monte, Lu. vi. 17-23 : originally for St. Sebastian, St. Hermes, and The Four Crowned Martyrs ; it became a Sarum Gospel for Many Martyrs, and thus for SS. Fabian and Sebastian, and for St. Denys and his companions.

Cum audieritis praelia, Lu. xxi. 9-19 : originally for SS. Marcellinus and Peter, then for Many Martyrs.

Attendite a fermento, Lu. xii. 1-8 : originally for SS. John and Paul and for St. Hippolytus, then for Many Martyrs.

Sedente Jesu super montem, Mt. xxiv. 3-13: originally for SS. Processus and Martinian, then for Many Martyrs. Part of this, *Videte ne quis* (5-13), was used in some early lists as an alternative Gospel for SS. Abdon and Sennen.

Vae vobis qui aedificatis, Lu. xi. 47-54: originally for SS. Cornelius and Cyprian ; then for Many Martyrs, when the commemoration of those Saints gave way to the observance of The Exaltation of the Holy Cross. It is available for St. Cyprian, or for the two bishops if they are commemorated on this day. At present

St. Cyprian's name alone appears in our Kalendar, and on the 26th, the day of a totally different Cyprian.

Egrediente Jesu, Mk. xiii. 1-13 : originally for SS. Gervasius and Protasius, and then for Many Martyrs.

Videte ne quis vos seducat, part of the previous Gospel beginning at verse 5 : originally used for St. Saturninus, then taken for Many Martyrs.

Nolite arbitrari, Mt. x. 34-42 : originally for SS. Gordian and Epimachus, and then for Many Martyrs. Part of this, *Qui amat patrem* (37-42), was one of the Gospels of St. Lawrence Day.

Homo quidam peregre, Mt. xxv. 14-23: originally for St. Marcellus, St. Mark (Oct. 7), St. Clement ; then for a Confessor, and used at Sarum for St. Nicholas, St. Wulfstan, St. David, St. Dunstan, St. Basil, St. Cuthbert, St. Martin, and also at York for St. Wilfrid, St. Aidan, St. Evurtius, St. Willibrord.

Videte, vigilate, Mk. xiii. 33-37 : not originally in the *Capitulare,* but used at Sarum for a Confessor, and allotted to St. Chad and St. Hugh.

Vigilate quia nescitis, Mt. xxiv. 42-47 : originally St. Silvester, St. Fabian, St. Eusebius, St. Calixtus, *i.e.* chiefly for Popes ; but used at Sarum for the Common of a Confessor, and allotted to St. Gregory, St. Patrick, St. Ambrose, St. Aldhelm, and St. Germanus, among others.

Vos estis sal (or *Vos estis lux,* at York), Mt. v. 13-19:

The Liturgical Gospels 39

not in the early *Capitulare*, but inserted before the tenth century, and used thence for a Confessor and Doctor, and therefore for St. Augustine and St. Jerome; and at Hereford and York for St. Ambrose.

Nemo accendit lucernam, Lu. xi. 33-36: originally the second Gospel for The Seven Brothers; then taken at Sarum for a Confessor and Abbot, and used for St. Leonard and St. Edward, and at York for St. Giles, St. Anthony and St. Botulf.

Sint lumbi,[1] Lu. xii. 35-40: originally for SS. Felix, Simplicius, etc., St. Agapitus and St. Martin; then at Sarum for Confessors, and available for St. Swithun, St. Remigius, besides St. Martin.

Misit Jesus duodecim, Mt. x. 5-8, or *In viam gentium*: not in the early *Capitulare*, but at Sarum for Confessors.

To these we may add:—

Hoc est praeceptum, Jo. xv. 12-16: originally for SS. Tiburtius, Valerian, and Maximus, and three other groups of Martyrs; used at Sarum not in the *Commune*, but for St. Barnabas; and so in the Prayer Book.

Loquente Jesu ad turbas, Mt. xii. 46-50: originally for St. Felicitas and her sons the Seven Brothers. It was taken at York and Hereford into the Common of Many Martyrs, but not at Sarum.

[1] Or *Nolite timere* (32-35) as used at York and Hereford for a Confessor.

§ 19

THESE lists represent (with two exceptions) the whole lists of Gospels for Saints' Days in the *Capitulare*, and the English medieval diocesan uses; and in following the order of the Sarum *Commune* above, we have noted in what way the Gospels should be allotted (according to English precedent) to the days which are more modern than the *Capitulare* but are included in the Prayer Book Kalendar. There remain the two unspecified Gospels to be noticed: and further there is the question of the allotment of Gospels to further festivals, not included in the English diocesan uses, but included in the Prayer Book Kalendar, or very likely to be so at any future revision.

1. *a.* The disappearance of the feast of St. Euplus (above, p. 33) left Jo. xvi. 20-23 unassigned to any Saint's Day. It would be specially suitable for a group of martyrs like those of Lyons and Vienne.

b. The old Gospel of SS. Nereus and Achilles is also unutilized (Mt. xix. 3-11). It would be specially appropriate to St. Columba, and also more appropriate to St. Cuthbert than the over-popular Gospel, *Homo quidam peregre*, which is usually allotted to him.

In the list from the *Commune* eight Gospels are mentioned, which are not, following old precedent, associated with any feast still to be continued. They are therefore available for other feasts which may be desirable now, though unadopted previously in the diocesan uses.

The Liturgical Gospels

Qui vos audit, (Lu. x. 16-20) would be appropriate for the two Founders of the chief orders of Friars, St. Dominick and St. Francis.

Cum audieritis praelia (Lu. xxi. 9-19) or in its shorter form *Ponite ergo in cordibus* (14-19), the old Gospel of St. Theodore and later of St. George, speaks about faithful witness going unscathed, and is suitable therefore for St. Athanasius, and for St. Anselm.

Attendite a fermento (Lu. xii 1-8) is suitable for Martyrs such as St. Irenaeus, and St. Justin, who bore written witness, and for SS. Ignatius and Polycarp, whom the Anglo-Saxon Church commemorated together on Feb. 1.

Sedente Jesu (Mt. xxiv. 3-18), telling of the tribulations of the Parousia, might well be allotted to St. Chrysostom, unless he is treated as a Doctor.

Egrediente Jesu (Mk. xiii. 1-13) is of the same theme, and is a longer form of *Videte ne quis* (ib. 5-13). It might be used for St Willibrord instead of *Homo quidam peregre*, for that belongs generally to a Confessor, not a Martyr.

Nolite arbitrari (Mt. x. 34-42) is only a longer form of the *Qui amat patrem* (ib. 37-42) of St. Lawrence.

Misit Jesus duodecim (Mt. x. 5-8) is a good Missionary Gospel, and suitable therefore for St. Ninian, St. Theodore, and for St. Columban, unless indeed he is treated as an Abbot and given (with St. Gilbert of Sempringham), the Gospel *Nemo accendit lucernam*.

Loquente Jesu (Mt. xii. 46-50) is a general Gospel suitable for those who have broken family ties for the following of Christ, *e.g.* for SS. Perpetua and Felicitas.

For any further Virgin Saints the two old Gospels must serve, while for Matrons such as St. Monnica, St. Margaret of Scotland, the Gospel *Dum perambularet*, the equivalent of *Intravit Jesus* (Lu. x. 38-42) (above, p. 26) is available and suitable.

§ 20.

SUMMING up the results thus reached we note:—

First, that six Gospels formerly in the *Commune* are now allotted to Red Letter Days in the Prayer Book. The Conversion of St. Paul, St. Mark, St. Barnabas, St Bartholomew, SS. Simon and Jude, and All Saints (cp. p. 27). The St. Mark's Gospel, *Ego sum vitis vera*, was formerly given also to other festivals in Eastertide, and would therefore be set down for St. George, St. Richard, and St. Alphege, if medieval practice were followed. It seems better, however, to disregard the medieval plan of having a special *Commune* for Eastertide, to keep *Ego sum vitis vera* for St. Mark's Day only, and to allot other Gospels to these Black Letter Days, choosing them as appropriate to the day itself rather than as appropriate to the Season of Eastertide in which they happen to fall. This Gospel then will be proper to St. Mark's Day; and every Red Letter Day will continue to have, as at present, a Proper Gospel. For St. George's Day a

The Liturgical Gospels 43

return should be made to the Gospel allotted in the *Capitulare*, *Ponite ergo*. St. Alphege might well share with St. Willibrord the Gospel *Egrediente Jesu*, and St. Richard share *Videte, vigilate*, with the other English Confessor Bishops, St. Chad and St. Hugh.

Secondly, a large number of Black Letter Days will have a proper Gospel; and there are a number of other cases in which a Gospel will be used only twice, so that a cross-reference from one place to another is all that seems needed.

Thirdly, there are Gospels which will be in more constant use and will therefore more conveniently form part of a *Commune*; e.g. *Si quis vult* for a Martyr; *Attendite a fermento* for martyred writers; *Si quis venit* for the three Martyr Kings; *Homo quidam nobilis* for certain Bishops; *Homo quidam peregre*, *Sint lumbi*, *Ponite ergo*, or *Cum audieritis*, *Videte, vigilate*, and *Vigilate quia* for a Bishop and Confessor; *Vos estis sal* for a Doctor; *Nemo accendit lucernam* for an Abbot; *Misit Jesus* for a Missionary; the two Gospels for Virgins; and *Dum perambularet* for Matrons.

We thus reach a scheme for the Saints' Days which provides (i) a proper Gospel for every Red Letter Day and for several Black Letter Days, (ii) other Gospels shared between two days, printed in the one place and referred to in the other, and (iii) a set of Common Gospels which are utilized more constantly. The scheme is not here fully worked out; for until the Kalendar is settled no final allotment can be made.

§ 21

THERE remains the question of Votive Masses. The *Capitulare* in its early form had a short list of these, comprising no more than twenty Gospels. The later developments introduced many more. Among the primitives are the following:—

>   Ordination of Priests. Mt. xxii. 42-47.
>   ,, ,, Deacons. Jo. xii. 24-26.
>   Dedication of a Church. Lu. vi. 43–48.
>   Veiling of Nuns. Mt. xxii. 1-14.
>   Marriage. Jo. iii. 27-29.
>   Service of the Dead. Jo. v. 21-24.
>   ,, ,, Jo. vi. 37-39.
>   ,, ,, Jo. vi. 48-54.
>   ,, ,, Jo. xi. 21-27.

In later medieval days the Gospel read at an Ordination (as also at the Veiling of a Nun) was that of the day, not a proper Gospel. The Prayer Book Ordinal, following Bucer, returned to the earlier plan, but adopted different passages. For the Dedication the later forms of the *Capitulare* provided an alternative, viz. Lu. xix. 1-9, and this, with an additional verse and a half, was adopted by the English diocesan uses. A similar process came about in regard to the nuptial Mass; but here the Gospel of the later *Capitulare*, Mt. xix.1-6, was the longer, while that of Sarum and Hereford began at verse 3, and York kept the older Gospel of the *Capitulare*. The Gospels for the Service of the Dead continued in use for the most part, and the second was retainéd in the First Prayer Book.

The remaining provision made by the *Capitulare*, in its earlier and later forms, seems hardly required for our present purpose, and need not therefore be considered. It does not meet modern requirements in such matters, *e.g.*, as a Harvest Thanksgiving, or a Coronation Mass. Drought, flood, war, and plague are provided for, journeys by sea and land, and more questionable contingencies such as the iniquities of judges and bishops. But for these we must refer the searcher to other sources: our attempt is limited to the consideration of the Ancient Gospel-books, so far as they are likely to affect the correction or enlargement of the series of Gospels in the Book of Common Prayer.

§ 22

These notes seem to indicate certain lines of reform and enrichment. On the one hand it is desirable that more of the Gospels should be read at the Eucharist through the year; on the other hand it is desirable, especially where there is a daily Celebration, that worshippers should be given greater variety of Scripture. This points especially to the provision of Gospels for the Black Letter Days and for the weekdays in Lent. But the details of enrichment, like the small details of reform, may be variously judged: the purpose of this tract is to raise questions rather than give a full and final answer to them.

A LIST OF LESSER FESTIVALS

JAN.	8. Lucian	⎫ In the Octave of
	13. Hilary	⎭ Epiphany.
	17. Anthony	*Nemo accendit.*
	18. Prisca	*Simile . . . thesauro.*
	19. Wulfstan	*Homo quidam peregre.*
	20. Fabian [and Sebastian]	*Vigilate.* [Lu. vi. 17-23.]
	21. Agnes	*Simile . . . decem.*
	22. Vincent	Jo. xii. 24-26.
	27. John Chrysostom	Mt. xxiv. 3-18.
	30. Charles K.	
FEB.	1. Ignatius and Polycarp	*Attendite a fermento.*
	3. Blaise	Mt. x. 26-32. Or as St. Boniface.
	4. Gilbert	*Nemo accendit.*
	5. Agatha	*Simile . . . decem.*
	14. Valentine	*Si quis vult.*
MARCH	1. David	*Homo quidam peregre.*
	2. Chad	*Videte, vigilate.*
	7. Perpetua and Felicitas	Mt. xii. 46-50.
	12. Gregory	*Vigilate.*
	17. Patrick	*Vigilate.*
	18. Edward K. and M.	*Si quis venit.*
	21. Benedict	*Nemo accendit.*
APRIL	3. Richard	*Videte, vigilate.*
	4. Ambrose	*Vigilate.*
	19. Alphege	As Willibrord.
	21. Anselm	*Cum audieritis.*
	23. George	*Cum audieritis.*
	24. Wilfrid	*Homo quidam peregre.*
MAY	2. Athanasius	*Cum audieritis.*
	3. Inv. of H. Cross	Jo. xii. 27-36.
	4. Monnica	*Dum perambularet.*
	6. John A.P.L.	As St. John's Day.

The Liturgical Gospels 47

MAY 19.	Dunstan	*Homo quidam peregre.*
25.	Aldhelm	*Vigilate.*
26.	Augustine of Canterbury	Lu. x. 1-7.
27.	Bede	*Vos estis sal.*
JUNE 1.	Nicomede	*Si quis vult.*
2.	Martyrs of Lyons	Jo. xvi. 20-22.
5.	Boniface [and his Comp.]	Mt. x. 23-26.
9.	Columba	Mt. xix. 3-11.
10.	Margaret Q.	*Dum perambularet.*
14.	Basil	*Homo quidam peregre.*
17.	Botulf	*Nemo accendit.*
20.	Tr. of Edward K. and M.	See March 18.
22.	Alban	*Si quis vult.*
28.	Irenaeus	*Attendite a fermento.*
JULY 2.	Visitation	Lu. i. 39-37.
4.	Tr. of Martin	See Nov. 11.
15.	Tr. of Swithun	*Sint lumbi.*
20.	Margaret	*Simile . . . thesauro.*
22.	Mary Magd.	Jo. xx. 11-18.
26.	Anne	*Dum perambularet.*
31.	Germanus and Lupus	*Vigilate.*
AUG. 1.	Lammas	As St. Peter's Octave.
4.	Dominick	Lu. x. 16-20.
5.	Oswald K. and M.	*Si quis venit.*
6.	Transfiguration	Mt. xvii. 1-9.
7.	Name of Jesus	Mt. i. 20-23.
10.	Lawrence	As St. Vincent.
28.	Augustine of Hippo	*Vos estis sal.*
29.	Beheading of John Baptist	Mk. vi. 17-29.
31.	Aidan	*Homo quidam peregre.*
SEPT. 1.	Giles	*Nemo accendit.*
4.	Tr. of Cuthbert	As St. Columba.
7.	Evurtius	*Homo quidam peregre.*
8.	Nativ. of B.V.M.	Lu. xi. 27-29.
13.	Cyprian and Cornelius	Lu. xi. 47-54.
14.	Exalt. of H. Cross	As the Invention.
16.	Ninian	*Misit Jesus.*
17.	Lambert	Mt. ix. 35-38.
19.	Theodore	*Misit Jesus.*
30.	Jerome	*Vos estis sal.*
OCT. 1.	Remigius	*Suit lumbi.*
4.	Francis	As St. Dominick.
6.	Faith	*Simile . . . thesauro.*

Oct.	9. Denys [and his Comp.]	As SS. Fabian and Sebastian.
	13. Tr. Edward Conf.	*Nemo accendit.*
	17. Etheldreda	*Simile . . . decem.*
	23. Justin M.	*Attendite a fermento.*
	25. Crispin [and Crispinian]	Mt. x. 16-22.
Nov.	6. Leonard	*Nemo accendit.*
	7. Willibrord	Mk. xiii. 1-13.
	11. Martin	*Sint lumbi.*
	13. Britius	*Homo quidam nobilis.*
	15. Machutus	*Homo quidam nobilis.*
	17. Hugh	*Videte, vigilate.*
	20. Edmund K..	*Si quis vult.*
	21. Columban	*Misit Jesus.*
	22. Cecilia	*Simile . . . decem.*
	23. Clement	As St. Machutus.
	25. Katharine	*Simile . . . thesauro.*
Dec.	6. Nicholas	*Homo quidam peregre.*
	8. Conception	As the Nativity.
	13. Lucy	*Simile . . . thesauro.*
	29. Thomas	*Homo quidam nobilis.*
	31. Silvester	*Vigilate.*